THE FAKE FACT

A KID'S INTRO TO MISINFORMATION

L FAIRLIGHT

THE FAKE FACT

A KID'S INTRO TO MISINFORMATION

L FAIRLIGHT

Sorry

I didn't used to like carrots.

But then my mum told me if you eat enough of them you can see in the dark.

Really?

When I asked her how she knew she said it was something her mum told her.

She even looked on the internet and this old poster popped up so we just believed it and didn't look any further...

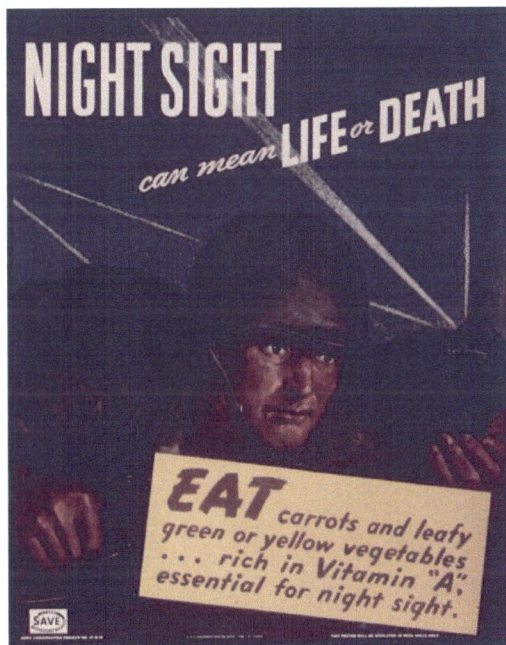

Image source: Wikimedia.org, public domain.

So I started eating LOADS of carrots.
I had them in my lunch box, after school, in the weekends...
Every time I was hungry I ate carrots, carrots, carrots!

I even told my friends.

Of course they believed me.

We started a carrot club and all ate carrots for lunch.

We're gonna be ninjas!

But even after several weeks I still couldn't see in the dark any better...

My friends started to ask more questions.

Was it really true?

Did I lie?

Was I playing a trick on them?

I had to prove to them I wasn't lying!

If I found out about that old poster that would prove I was right!

Maybe we just weren't eating enough carrots!

I found out a lot about carrots.

I learned they are a source of vitamin A.

I learned they usually take 70 to 80 days to grow.

I learned they can be all sorts of colours. Even purple.

And I also found out that the fact my mum had told me about carrots was **NOT TRUE!**

It turns out that was a trick made up in World War Two.

The British made up the lie to fool their enemies and waste their time...

But then a lot of British people heard it and believed it too...

Carrots were pretty popular back then anyway. They even ate them on sticks instead of ice-blocks because sugar was hard to get. (That's something else I learned about carrots).

Sorry

It is true that carrots are
good for your eye health...

But there is **no evidence** that they
will make you see in the dark.

The fake fact travelled from back then... to my grandma... to my mum...

TO ME!

And from me the fake fact travelled to...

...my whole class!

I said sorry to my class. Some of them were a bit mad they couldn't see in the dark like ninjas. But they got over it eventually.

And I learned so many interesting things about carrots I kind of like them for different reasons now anyway.

I also learned a lot about how information travels and how to trace it back where it comes from.

I won't be tricked again so easily.

DISCUSSION POINTS

A lot of fake facts are believable because they have **a grain of truth.**

Watch how the fake fact about carrots came about:

TRUE: Carrots contain beta-carotene which helps you produce Vitamin A.

TRUE: Having low levels of Vitamin A is linked with vision problems.

SIMPLIFIED

TRUE: Carrots are good for healthy eyes.

EXAGGERATED

FALSE: Eating carrots will give you sharper vision and make you see in the dark.

What do you need to watch out for to identify a fake fact?
What else have you heard that might be a fake fact?

DISCUSSION POINTS

How do you know what you have heard is true?

How do you check if the person making the claim is reliable?

If you hear something that you think is wrong, what do you do?

If you have told someone something and you later find out it was a fake fact, how do you deal with it?

DISCUSSION POINTS

Why do people make up fake facts? What do they get out of it?
Are they trying to trick someone? Sell something?
What questions do you need to ask to figure out if they have a motive to lie?

Some people will tell you things because they believe it.

Would you get mad at them if they tell you something that isn't true?

They didn't do it on purpose... How do you deal with it?

DISCUSSION POINTS

It can be hard to admit you were wrong. A lot of people will look for information to prove them right rather than information that could prove them wrong. They will also **weigh information** that agrees with them as more reliable than information that disagrees. This is called **confirmation bias.**

If you do this you can become more convinced that a fake fact is true, regardless of the evidence.

How would you deal with those feelings? Has there been a time you've been wrong about something before?

I really wanted it to be true...

I didn't want to tell my friends I was wrong.

DISCUSSION POINTS

FOR OLDER KIDS

Information can travel a long way. To check facts you need to trace it back to the **primary source.**

PRIMARY SOURCE

The original or primary source of the information might be a research paper by a scientist.

Published research papers are peer reviewed and checked over by other scientists. This might talk about beta-carotene and Vitamin A.

A lot of these papers might seem really boring for the average person and take a long time to read, so a lot of people won't bother reading them.

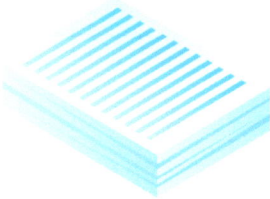

SECONDARY SOURCE

A secondary source might be a newspaper. This has been written by a journalist who has read the paper, but he has simplified it for the average person to read. It might have a snappy headline like "Carrots help your eyes!"

It also might have a mistake because he is not a scientist and it wont be peer reviewed by a scientist who knows the research. It might be checked by an editor but he won't have read the research paper either.

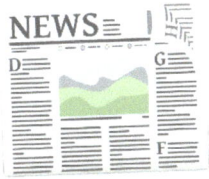

TERTIARY SOURCE

A tertiary source is another step away from the source of the fact. This might be a vlogger who read the newspaper article and has based all her information off that, even if it contained mistakes. They might also make entirely new mistakes.

What are some other primary, secondary and tertiary sources?

DISCUSSION POINTS

FOR OLDER KIDS

Identifying bias can be really tricky. Even different newspapers will put their own spin on articles and interpret them according to their values.

This can make some news look contradictory - one must be true and one must be wrong, right?

It is possible that an article could be wrong, but it is also possible that the two articles are picking different things to focus on and simplifying them - so you don't get the full picture like you would get from reading the full source information.

Try picking a topic that interests you, and read a few different articles from different sources. See if you can identify the bias in the coverage.

ACTIVITY EXAMPLE

Look at these four headlines. Is there a worker shortage or not?

Worker shortage could put squeeze on apple season

No quick fix for New Zealand's labour market mess

Hospo union says there's a wage shortage, not a labour shortage

The great New Zealand labour shortage might not exist

It might be helpful to look at different articles as being a conversation in a room between people with different opinions and experiences.

Rather than telling you what to think or what to believe, you can look at news articles as fostering a conversation, especially when it comes to big complicated issues.

It is important to read widely to see a lot of different opinions and to think critically about what information sources they are using and if they are simplifying the facts or presenting them with a bias. For example, people in a city might experience a labour shortage differently from people in rural areas.

If you read more, you will know more sides of the conversation. Where will you look to find different opinions, and how will you test them for reliability and bias?

ABOUT CARROTS IN WW2

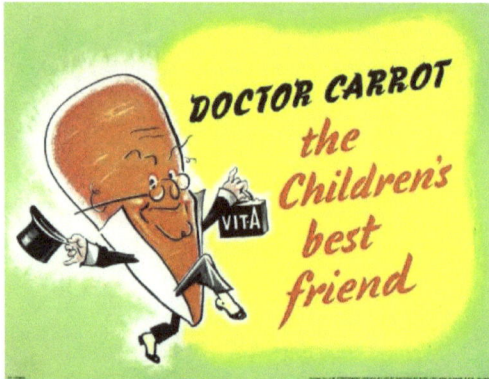

DOCTOR CARROT
the Children's best friend

Image source: Wikimedia.org, public domain.

Propaganda about carrots from the British Ministry of Food was well documented.

It was partially in response to an oversupply in carrots, and citizens were recommended to plant extra rows of vegetables to save strain on importing other food. Mascots like 'Dr Carrot' ad Walt Disney's 'Carroty George' were also useful in popularising carrots.

The propaganda aimed at Germany was also intended to distract them from discovering the radar technology that the British airforce was using for navigation. The misinformation about carrots helping you to see in the dark was also very attractive to British citizens, as during the air raids there were city wide blackouts. These blackouts meant that enemy planes could not see where to drop bombs as there were no lights allowed - but this also caused a lot of accidents!

For more information on carrots, check out **carrotmuseum.co.uk**

I'm a protective food
Says 'POTATO PETE'

Image source: Wikimedia.org, public domain.

Potatoes also got their own mascot. They were kind of cute!

MORE TOPICS TO TALK ABOUT

App permissions - when you download apps, what information and access are you allowing them to have?

Strangers on the internet - how do you know they are who they say they are?

Protecting your information - being aware of what you put online (ie: school logos in photos) and the danger of fun quizzes that ask common security questions.

Suspicious links and scams and what to do if you spot them.

In app purchases - can you recognize when you are buying things with game coins or real dollars?

Parental safety controls - what ones will be helpful to keep safe, and when will they come off?

Phone blackout times/digital detoxes - How much time is reasonable to be on your phone per day or per week? Do you need structure to help you with your habits?

What do you do if you come across something that makes you uncomfortable?

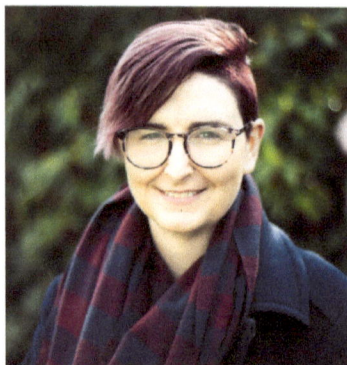

FROM THE AUTHOR

Thank you for buying my book and congratulations on being an awesome parent (or teacher) for taking some proactive steps to teach your kids about cyber-safety and digital literacy.

Kids are getting access to devices younger and younger, and the odds are they'll find things out through their friends before you even know it which is why it's so important to get in early. These are conversations we need to have again and again, getting more in depth as they age and can think more critically about different issues.

I do have more books planned in this series, so keep your eye out. As a self-published author I'll also be using the profits from these books to pay for illustrations for the next so I do appreciate each sale. If you are a school and want to enquire about making copies of pages for classroom use, please email me at laurawolfauthor@gmail.com

You can also ask your local library to stock this book.

OTHER BOOKS IN THE SERIES